EVERYDAY

AIR FRYER

COOKBOOK

Easy and flavourful Recipes
for healthy Cooking
Throughout the week

JOSEPH J. EASLEY

1

TABLE OF CONTENTS

Introduction

Tips for Getting the Most Out of Your Air Fryer

AIR FRYER MAIN DISHES
- Air Fryer Salmon
- Air Fryer Chicken Thighs
- Air Fryer Beef Meatballs
- Air Fryer Pork Chops
- Air Fryer Steak Fajitas
- Air Fryer Shrimp Scampi
- Air Fryer Chicken Parmesan
- Air Fryer Pork Tenderloin

AIR FRYER VEGETABLE SIDES
- Air Fryer Brussels Sprouts
- Air Fryer Asparagus
- Air Fryer Sweet Potato Fries
- Air Fryer Cauliflower
- Air Fryer Broccoli
- Air Fryer Green Beans
- Air Fryer Roasted Potatoes
- Air Fryer Eggplant Fries

AIR FRYER DESSERTS
- Air Fryer Apple Pie Bites
- Air Fryer Donuts
- Air Fryer Churros
- Air Fryer Chocolate Chip Cookies
- Air Fryer Cinnamon Rolls

INTRODUCTION

Tips for Getting the Most Out of Your Air Fryer

Now that you've got your shiny new air fryer, how can you make sure you're using it to its full potential? Here are some tips to help you get the most out of this versatile kitchen appliance:

Start with the Right Size

Air fryers come in a variety of sizes, from compact models that can handle 2-3 servings to larger ones that can cook up to 6 portions at once. When choosing an air fryer, think about how many people you'll typically be cooking for. Err on the side of a slightly larger capacity to give yourself more flexibility.

Preheat for Best Results

Just like a traditional oven, preheating your air fryer for 3-5 minutes before adding food helps ensure even, crispy cooking. This small step makes a big difference in the final texture of fried foods.

Use the Right Cooking Spray

Invest in a high-quality olive oil or avocado oil cooking spray. These lightweight sprays help food crisp up without adding a lot of extra fat and calories like regular cooking oils can.

Don't Overcrowd the Basket

Resist the urge to stuff your air fryer basket to the max. Overcrowding will cause foods to steam instead of getting that desired crispy texture. Cook in batches if needed to ensure adequate airflow around each item.

Shake or Flip Halfway

For best results, open the air fryer basket and shake or flip food items halfway through the cooking time. This promotes even browning on all sides.

Get Creative with Accessories

Air fryer accessories like baking pans, skewers, and silicone molds open up a world of cooking possibilities beyond just frying. Experiment to find your favorite add-ons.

AIR FRYER
BREAKFAST RECIPES

AIR FRYER BREAKFAST POTATOES

Ingredients:

- 2 lbs russet or Yukon gold potatoes, peeled and cubed into 1-inch pieces
- 2 tbsp olive oil
- 1 tsp garlic powder
- 1 tsp paprika
- 1 tsp dried oregano
- 1/2 tsp salt
- 1/4 tsp black pepper

Method:

1. First, preheat your air fryer to 400°F.
2. In a big bowl, toss the cubed potatoes with the olive oil and all the seasonings. Make sure the potatoes are evenly coated.
3. Working in batches if needed, add the seasoned potatoes to your air fryer basket in a single layer.
4. Air fry for 12-15 minutes, shaking the basket or flipping the potatoes halfway

through, until they're crispy and golden brown.

5. Serve these air fryer breakfast potatoes hot, optionally garnished with some chopped parsley.

Tips:

- For even crispier potatoes, try soaking the cubed potatoes in cold water for 30 minutes before cooking. This removes excess starch.
- Feel free to mix in some diced onions, peppers, or other veggies for extra flavor.
- Top with shredded cheese, crumbled bacon, or a fried egg to make it a complete breakfast.

AIR FRYER FRENCH TOAST STICKS

Ingredients:

- Thick-sliced bread cut the slices into 3-inch sticks
- 3 large eggs for the batter.

- 1/2 cup of milk
- 1 teaspoon of vanilla extract
- 1/2 teaspoon of ground cinnamon
- Pinch of salt

Method:

- In a shallow bowl, whisk together the eggs, milk, vanilla, cinnamon, and salt until well combined.
- Dip each breadstick into the egg batter, turning to coat all sides.
- Preheat your air fryer to 380°F.
- Working in batches, carefully place the battered french toast sticks in a single layer in the air fryer basket.
- Air fry for 5-7 minutes, flipping halfway through, until golden brown and crispy.
- Repeat with remaining bread sticks, working in batches as needed.
- Serve the air fryer french toast sticks hot, with your favorite toppings like maple syrup, powdered sugar, or fresh fruit.

Tips:

- For extra crispy sticks, try spraying the basket with a bit of nonstick cooking spray before adding the battered bread.
- Jazz up the batter by adding a splash of orange juice or a pinch of nutmeg.
- Make it a meal by serving the french toast sticks with scrambled eggs, bacon, or sausage on the side.

AIR FRYER BREAKFAST BURRITOS

Ingredients:

- Tortillas - Use large flour tortillas or wraps, about 8-10 inches in size.
- Eggs - Scramble 8-10 large eggs with a splash of milk and a pinch of salt and pepper.
- Potatoes - Dice 1-2 russet or Yukon gold potatoes and air fry until crispy.
- Meat - Cook and crumble 1/2 lb of breakfast sausage or crisp up some bacon.

- Cheese - Grated cheddar or Mexican blend cheese.
- Optional extras: Diced onions, bell peppers, salsa, hot sauce.

Method:

- Lay a tortilla out flat on a clean surface. Spoon some of the scrambled eggs down the center, leaving a couple inches of space on the edges.
- Top the eggs with some of the crispy air fried potatoes, crumbled sausage or bacon, and shredded cheese.
- Fold the bottom of the tortilla up over the filling, then fold in the sides and continue rolling tightly into a burrito shape.
- Place the burrito seam-side down in your preheated air fryer basket.
- Air fry at 370°F for 8-10 minutes, flipping halfway, until the tortilla is golden brown and crispy.

- Repeat with remaining ingredients to make 4-6 burritos.

Serving:

Serve the hot air fryer breakfast burritos immediately, with any desired toppings or dipping sauces on the side. They're fantastic with salsa, guacamole, sour cream, or hot sauce.

AIR FRYER BACON AND EGGS

Ingredients:

- Bacon - 6-8 slices of your favorite bacon
- Eggs - 4-6 large eggs
- Salt and pepper to taste

Method:

1. Preheat your air fryer to 400°F.
2. Lay the bacon slices in a single layer in the air fryer basket. Cook for 8-10 minutes, flipping halfway, until crispy.

3. Remove the cooked bacon from the air fryer and set aside on a plate lined with paper towels to drain any excess grease.

4. Crack the eggs directly into the air fryer basket, being careful not to overcrowd. You may need to work in batches depending on the size of your basket.

5. Air fry the eggs for 3-5 minutes, until the whites are set but the yolks are still runny. Season with salt and pepper.

6. Serve the air fried bacon and eggs hot, with the eggs cooked to your desired doneness. For firmer yolks, air fry a minute or two longer.

Tips:

- For crispier bacon, try preheating the air fryer basket before adding the bacon.
- Adjust the cooking times as needed based on how you like your eggs - less time for runny yolks, more for harder set.

- Get creative with mix-ins like cheese, herbs, or hot sauce to customize your air fryer breakfast.
- Serve with toast, hash browns, or other breakfast sides for a complete meal.

AIR FRYER BREAKFAST CASSEROLE

Ingredients:

- 8 large eggs
- 1/2 lb breakfast sausage, cooked and crumbled
- 2 cups diced russet potatoes (about 1 large potato)
- 1 cup shredded cheddar cheese
- 1/4 cup milk
- 1 tsp salt
- 1/2 tsp black pepper

Method:

1. Preheat your air fryer to 350°F.
2. In a large mixing bowl, whisk together the eggs, milk, salt, and pepper until well combined.
3. Stir in the cooked sausage, diced potatoes, and shredded cheese until everything is evenly distributed.
4. Grease a 6-inch oven-safe baking dish or ramekin that will fit in your air fryer basket. Pour the egg mixture into the prepared dish.
5. Place the dish in the preheated air fryer basket and cook for 18-22 minutes, until the center is set and no longer jiggles.
6. Remove the casserole from the air fryer and let it cool for 5 minutes before slicing and serving.

Tips:

- Use a baking dish or ramekin that fits snugly in your air fryer basket for even cooking.
- Dice the potatoes into small 1/4-inch cubes so they cook through fully.
- Swap the sausage for bacon or ham if desired.
- Add in diced onions, peppers, spinach or other veggies to customize the flavors.
- Serve the air fryer breakfast casserole with salsa, avocado, or a dollop of sour cream on top.

AIR FRYER BREAKFAST HASH

Ingredients:

- 1 lb russet potatoes, diced into 1/2-inch cubes
- 1/2 lb breakfast sausage, cooked and crumbled
- 1 bell pepper, diced

- 1 small onion, diced
- 2 tbsp olive oil
- 1 tsp salt
- 1/2 tsp black pepper
- 1/2 tsp paprika
- 4 eggs (optional)

Method:

1. Preheat your air fryer to 400°F.
2. In a large bowl, toss the diced potatoes with the olive oil, salt, pepper, and paprika until evenly coated.
3. Transfer the seasoned potatoes to the air fryer basket in a single layer. Cook for 12-15 minutes, shaking the basket halfway, until the potatoes are crispy and golden brown.
4. Remove the potatoes from the air fryer and transfer to a large bowl. Add the cooked sausage, diced bell pepper, and diced onion. Toss to combine.

5. Spread the hash mixture back into the air fryer basket in an even layer. Cook for an additional 5-7 minutes, until the veggies are tender.
6. Optional: Create 4 wells in the hash and carefully crack the eggs into them. Air fry for 3-5 minutes, until the eggs are cooked to your desired doneness.
7. Serve the air fryer breakfast hash immediately, garnished with fresh chopped parsley if desired.

Tips:

- For crispier potatoes, soak the diced potatoes in cold water for 30 minutes before patting dry and seasoning.
- Use a mix of bell peppers for more color and flavor.
- Customize with other veggies like mushrooms, spinach, or tomatoes.
- Top with shredded cheese, avocado, salsa, or a dollop of sour cream.

AIR FRYER BREAKFAST HASH

Ingredients:

- 1 lb russet potatoes, diced into 1/2-inch cubes
- 1/2 lb breakfast sausage, cooked and crumbled
- 1 bell pepper, diced
- 1 small onion, diced
- 2 tbsp olive oil
- 1 tsp salt
- 1/2 tsp black pepper
- 1/2 tsp paprika
- 4 eggs (optional)

Method:

1. Preheat your air fryer to 400°F.
2. In a large bowl, toss the diced potatoes with the olive oil, salt, pepper, and paprika until evenly coated.
3. Transfer the seasoned potatoes to the air fryer basket in a single layer. Cook for

12-15 minutes, shaking the basket halfway, until the potatoes are crispy and golden brown.

4. Remove the potatoes from the air fryer and transfer to a large bowl. Add the cooked sausage, diced bell pepper, and diced onion. Toss to combine.
5. Spread the hash mixture back into the air fryer basket in an even layer. Cook for an additional 5-7 minutes, until the veggies are tender.
6. Optional: Create 4 wells in the hash and carefully crack the eggs into them. Air fry for 3-5 minutes, until the eggs are cooked to your desired doneness.
7. Serve the air fryer breakfast hash immediately, garnished with fresh chopped parsley if desired.

Tips:

- For crispier potatoes, soak the diced potatoes in cold water for 30 minutes before patting dry and seasoning.
- Use a mix of bell peppers for more color and flavor.
- Customize with other veggies like mushrooms, spinach, or tomatoes.
- Top with shredded cheese, avocado, salsa, or a dollop of sour cream.

AIR FRYER BREAKFAST SANDWICHES

Ingredients:

- 4 English muffins, split in half
- 4 large eggs
- 4 slices cheese (cheddar, American, or Swiss)
- 4 cooked breakfast sausage patties, bacon slices, or ham slices
- Butter or nonstick cooking spray

Method:

1. Preheat your air fryer to 370°F.
2. Lightly butter or spray the insides of the English muffin halves. Place the muffin bottoms in a single layer in the air fryer basket.
3. Crack the eggs directly onto the muffin bottoms, being careful not to let them run together. Top each egg with a slice of cheese.
4. Place the cooked breakfast meat (sausage, bacon, or ham) on top of the cheese.
5. Add the muffin tops to the air fryer basket, placing them directly on top of the assembled sandwiches.
6. Air fry for 5-7 minutes, until the eggs are cooked through and the cheese is melted.
7. Carefully remove the breakfast sandwiches from the air fryer and serve immediately.

Tips:

- For runny yolks, cook the eggs for 5 minutes. For fully cooked yolks, cook for 6-7 minutes.
- Customize with different cheese varieties or breakfast meat.
- Add a smear of butter, jam, or honey to the muffin tops.
- Cook the sausage, bacon or ham in the air fryer first before assembling the sandwiches.
- Make a big batch and wrap individually to reheat later for a quick on-the-go breakfast.

AIR FRYER BREAKFAST PIZZA

Ingredients:

- 1 can (8 oz) refrigerated crescent roll dough
- 6 large eggs, scrambled

- 1/2 lb breakfast sausage, cooked and crumbled
- 1 cup shredded cheddar cheese
- 2 tbsp milk
- 1/2 tsp salt
- 1/4 tsp black pepper

Method:

1. Preheat your air fryer to 350°F.
2. On a lightly floured surface, unroll the crescent roll dough and press it into a 6-inch circle, pinching the seams together to seal.
3. Transfer the dough circle to a lightly greased air fryer-safe baking dish or pan that will fit in your air fryer basket.
4. In a medium bowl, whisk together the scrambled eggs, milk, salt, and pepper until well combined.
5. Pour the egg mixture over the crescent roll dough, then sprinkle the cooked sausage

crumbles and shredded cheddar cheese on top.

6. Air fry for 12-15 minutes, until the crust is golden brown and the cheese is melted and bubbly.

7. Remove the breakfast pizza from the air fryer and let it cool for 5 minutes before slicing and serving.

Tips:

- Use a store-bought canned pizza crust or homemade dough if you don't want to use crescent rolls.
- Customize with your favorite breakfast toppings like bacon, ham, onions, peppers, etc.
- Brush the crust with a little melted butter or olive oil before air frying for extra crispy edges.
- Serve the breakfast pizza with a side of salsa, hot sauce, or sour cream for dipping.

- Leftovers can be reheated in the air fryer for 3-4 minutes to crisp up the crust again.
- Air Fryer Appetizers & Snacks

AIR FRYER

APPETIZERS & SNACKS

AIR FRYER CHICKEN WINGS

Ingredients:

- 2 lbs chicken wings, drumettes and flats separated
- 2 tbsp olive oil
- 1 tsp salt
- 1/2 tsp black pepper
- 1/2 tsp garlic powder
- 1/2 tsp paprika

Method:

1. Preheat your air fryer to 400°F.
2. Pat the chicken wings dry with paper towels and place them in a large bowl. Drizzle with the olive oil and sprinkle with the salt, pepper, garlic powder, and paprika. Toss to coat the wings evenly.
3. Working in batches if needed, arrange the wings in a single layer in the air fryer basket, making sure they aren't touching.

4. Air fry for 20-25 minutes, flipping the wings halfway through, until they are crispy and cooked through. The internal temperature should reach 165°F.

5. Remove the wings from the air fryer and toss them with your favorite sauce, if desired. Some great options include buffalo, barbecue, honey garlic, or lemon pepper.

6. Serve the air fryer chicken wings immediately, garnished with chopped parsley or scallions if desired. Enjoy!

Tips:

- For extra crispy skin, pat the wings very dry before seasoning.
- Cook the wings in a single layer with space between them for best results.
- Toss the cooked wings in sauce while they're still hot so it adheres well.
- Air fry in batches if needed to avoid overcrowding the basket.

- Leftover wings can be reheated in the air fryer for 3-4 minutes to crisp them up again.

AIR FRYER MOZZARELLA STICKS

Ingredients:

- 8 mozzarella cheese sticks, cut in half crosswise
- 1/2 cup all-purpose flour
- 2 large eggs, beaten
- 1 cup panko breadcrumbs
- 1/2 cup grated parmesan cheese
- 1 tsp garlic powder
- 1/2 tsp salt
- 1/4 tsp black pepper
- Marinara sauce, for serving (optional)

Method:

1. Preheat your air fryer to 400°F.
2. Set up 3 shallow dishes - one with the flour, one with the beaten eggs, and one

with the panko, parmesan, garlic powder, salt, and pepper mixed together.

3. Working with one piece of cheese at a time, dip the mozzarella stick first in the flour, then the egg, and finally the panko-parmesan mixture, pressing gently to help it adhere.
4. Carefully place the breaded mozzarella sticks in a single layer in the air fryer basket, making sure they aren't touching.
5. Air fry for 6-8 minutes, flipping halfway through, until the bread is golden brown and crispy.
6. Remove the mozzarella sticks from the air fryer and serve immediately with marinara sauce for dipping, if desired.

Tips:

- Freeze the mozzarella sticks for 30 minutes before breading to help them hold their shape.

- Work in batches to avoid overcrowding the air fryer basket.
- Spray the breaded mozzarella sticks lightly with cooking oil for extra crispy results.
- Try different seasoning blends in the breadcrumb mixture like Italian herbs or ranch seasoning.
- Reheat leftover mozzarella sticks in the air fryer for 2-3 minutes to recrisp the breading.

AIR FRYER ONION RINGS

Ingredients:

- 2 large onions, sliced into 1/2-inch thick rings
- 1 cup all-purpose flour
- 2 large eggs, beaten
- 1 1/2 cups panko breadcrumbs
- 1 tsp garlic powder
- 1 tsp paprika
- 1/2 tsp salt

- 1/4 tsp black pepper
- Cooking spray

Method:

1. Preheat your air fryer to 400°F.
2. Separate the onion slices into rings and place them in a large bowl of cold water to soak for 30 minutes. This helps remove the harsh onion flavor.
3. Drain the onion rings and pat them dry thoroughly with paper towels.
4. Set up three shallow dishes - one with the flour, one with the beaten eggs, and one with the panko, garlic powder, paprika, salt, and pepper mixed together.
5. Working in batches, dip the onion rings first in the flour, then the egg, and finally the panko mixture, pressing gently to adhere.
6. Lightly spray the air fryer basket with cooking spray. Arrange the breaded onion

rings in a single layer, making sure they don't touch.

7. Air fry for 8-10 minutes, flipping halfway through, until golden brown and crispy.

8. Remove the onion rings from the air fryer and serve immediately, garnished with chopped parsley if desired.

Tips:

- Soak the onion rings in ice water for even crisper results.
- Use a combination of panko and regular breadcrumbs for extra crunch.
- Spray the onion rings lightly with cooking oil for an even crispier texture.
- Work in batches to avoid overcrowding the air fryer basket.
- Reheat leftover onion rings in the air fryer for 2-3 minutes to recrisp them.

AIR FRYER FRIED PICKLES

Ingredients:

- 1 (16 oz) jar dill pickle chips, drained and patted dry
- 1/2 cup all-purpose flour
- 2 large eggs, beaten
- 1 cup panko breadcrumbs
- 1 tsp garlic powder
- 1/2 tsp onion powder
- 1/2 tsp smoked paprika
- 1/2 tsp salt
- 1/4 tsp black pepper
- Ranch dressing, for serving (optional)

Method:

1. Preheat your air fryer to 400°F.
2. Set up three shallow dishes - one with the flour, one with the beaten eggs, and one with the panko, garlic powder, onion powder, smoked paprika, salt, and pepper mixed together.

3. Working in batches, dip the pickle chips first in the flour, then the egg, and finally the panko mixture, pressing gently to adhere.
4. Arrange the breaded pickle chips in a single layer in the air fryer basket, making sure they aren't touching.
5. Air fry for 6-8 minutes, flipping halfway through, until the bread is golden brown and crispy.
6. Remove the fried pickles from the air fryer and serve immediately, with ranch dressing for dipping if desired.

Tips:

- Pat the pickle chips very dry before breading for maximum crispiness.
- Use dill or spicy pickle chips for extra flavor.
- For extra crispy results, lightly spray the breaded pickles with cooking oil.

- Work in batches to avoid overcrowding the air fryer basket.
- Reheat leftovers in the air fryer for 2-3 minutes to recrisp them.

AIR FRYER JALAPEÑO POPPERS

Ingredients:

- 12 jalapeño peppers, halved lengthwise and seeded
- 4 oz cream cheese, softened
- 1/2 cup shredded cheddar cheese
- 2 tbsp chopped fresh cilantro
- 1/4 tsp garlic powder
- 1/4 tsp salt
- 1/8 tsp black pepper
- 1/2 cup panko breadcrumbs
- 2 tbsp grated parmesan cheese
- Cooking spray

Method:

1. Preheat your air fryer to 400°F.

2. In a small bowl, mix together the cream cheese, cheddar cheese, cilantro, garlic powder, salt, and pepper until well combined.

3. Spoon the cheese mixture evenly into the jalapeño halves.

4. In another bowl, mix together the panko and parmesan.

5. Lightly spray the air fryer basket with cooking spray. Working in batches, place the stuffed jalapeño halves in the basket in a single layer. Spray the tops lightly with cooking spray.

6. Air fry for 8-10 minutes, flipping halfway through, until the tops are golden brown and crispy.

7. Remove the jalapeño poppers from the air fryer and serve immediately, garnished with extra cilantro if desired.

Tips:

- Wear gloves when handling the jalapeños to avoid burning your hands.
- For less heat, use milder peppers like Anaheim or banana peppers.
- Add a sprinkle of smoked paprika or chili powder to the panko mixture for extra flavor.
- Try different cheese combinations like pepper jack or gouda.
- Reheat any leftover poppers in the air fryer for 2-3 minutes to recrisp the breading.

AIR FRYER ZUCCHINI FRIES

Ingredients:

- 2 medium zucchinis, cut into 1/2-inch thick fry shapes
- 1/2 cup all-purpose flour
- 2 large eggs, beaten
- 1 cup panko breadcrumbs

- 1 tsp garlic powder
- 1 tsp dried oregano
- 1/2 tsp salt
- 1/4 tsp black pepper
- Cooking spray

Method:

1. Preheat your air fryer to 400°F.
2. Set up three shallow dishes - one with the flour, one with the beaten eggs, and one with the panko, garlic powder, oregano, salt, and pepper mixed together.
3. Working in batches, dip the zucchini fries first in the flour, then the egg, and finally the panko mixture, pressing gently to adhere.
4. Arrange the breaded zucchini fries in a single layer in the air fryer basket, making sure they aren't touching. Lightly spray the tops with cooking spray.

5. Air fry for 10-12 minutes, flipping halfway through, until the fries are golden brown and crispy.
6. Remove the zucchini fries from the air fryer and serve immediately, garnished with chopped parsley if desired. Enjoy!

Tips:

- Pat the zucchini fries very dry before breading for maximum crispiness.
- For extra crispy results, spritz the fries lightly with cooking spray before and during air frying.
- Try using different seasoning blends like Cajun, Italian, or ranch.
- Work in batches to avoid overcrowding the air fryer basket.
- Reheat leftovers in the air fryer for 2-3 minutes to recrisp them.

AIR FRYER CAULIFLOWER BITES

Ingredients:

- 1 head of cauliflower, cut into 1-inch florets
- 2 tbsp olive oil
- 1 tsp garlic powder
- 1 tsp paprika
- 1/2 tsp salt
- 1/4 tsp black pepper

Method:

1. Preheat your air fryer to 400°F.
2. In a large bowl, toss the cauliflower florets with the olive oil, garlic powder, paprika, salt, and pepper until evenly coated.
3. Working in batches, arrange the seasoned cauliflower florets in a single layer in the air fryer basket. Make sure not to overcrowd.

4. Air fry for 10-12 minutes, shaking the basket halfway through, until the cauliflower is golden brown and crispy.
5. Remove the air fried cauliflower bites from the basket and serve immediately, garnished with chopped parsley or your favorite dipping sauce if desired.

Tips:

- For extra crispy results, pat the cauliflower florets very dry before tossing with oil and seasoning.
- Try different spice blends like Cajun, Ranch, or Buffalo.
- Toss the hot cauliflower bites in a little Parmesan cheese or lemon juice for extra flavor.
- Reheat any leftovers in the air fryer for 2-3 minutes to recrisp them.

AIR FRYER CHICKEN TENDERS

Ingredients:

- 1 lb chicken tenderloins
- 1 cup all-purpose flour
- 2 large eggs, beaten
- 1 cup panko breadcrumbs
- 1 tsp garlic powder
- 1 tsp paprika
- 1 tsp salt
- 1/2 tsp black pepper
- Cooking spray

Method:

1. Preheat your air fryer to 400°F.
2. Set up three shallow dishes - one with the flour, one with the beaten eggs, and one with the panko, garlic powder, paprika, salt, and pepper mixed together.
3. Working in batches, dip the chicken tenders first in the flour, then the egg, and

finally the panko mixture, pressing gently to adhere.

4. Arrange the breaded chicken tenders in a single layer in the air fryer basket, making sure they aren't touching. Lightly spray the tops with cooking spray.

5. Air fry for 10-12 minutes, flipping halfway through, until the chicken is cooked through and the breading is golden brown and crispy.

6. Remove the air fryer chicken tenders from the basket and serve immediately, garnished with chopped parsley if desired. Enjoy!

Tips:

- For extra crispy results, double dip the chicken in the egg and panko mixture.
- Try different seasoning blends like Ranch, Buffalo, or Cajun.

- Serve the chicken tenders with your favorite dipping sauces like honey mustard, BBQ, or ranch.
- Work in batches to avoid overcrowding the air fryer basket.
- Reheat any leftovers in the air fryer for 2-3 minutes to recrisp them.

AIR FRYER

MAIN DISHES

AIR FRYER SALMON

Ingredients:

- 4 (6 oz) salmon fillets, skin-on or skinless
- 2 tbsp olive oil
- 1 tsp garlic powder
- 1 tsp paprika
- 1 tsp salt
- 1/2 tsp black pepper

Methods:

1. Preheat your air fryer to 400°F.
2. Pat the salmon fillets dry with paper towels and place them in a single layer in a shallow baking dish or plate.
3. In a small bowl, mix together the olive oil, garlic powder, paprika, salt, and pepper. Brush or rub this seasoning mixture all over the top and sides of the salmon fillets.
4. Carefully transfer the seasoned salmon fillets to the air fryer basket, arranging

them in a single layer with a little space between each piece.

5. Air fry for 8-12 minutes, flipping the fillets halfway through, until the salmon is opaque and flakes easily with a fork. The internal temperature should reach 145°F.

6. Remove the air fryer salmon from the basket and serve immediately, garnished with lemon wedges, chopped parsley, or your favorite sauce or glaze.

Tips:

- For extra crispy skin, pat the salmon very dry before seasoning.
- Try different spice blends like Cajun, lemon-pepper, or teriyaki.
- Brush the salmon with a little honey, maple syrup, or sweet chili sauce towards the end of cooking for a delicious glaze.
- Air fry the salmon in batches if needed to avoid overcrowding the basket.

- Reheat any leftover salmon in the air fryer for 2-3 minutes to recrisp the exterior.

AIR FRYER CHICKEN THIGHS

Ingredients:

- 6 bone-in, skin-on chicken thighs
- 2 tbsp olive oil
- 1 tsp garlic powder
- 1 tsp paprika
- 1 tsp salt
- 1/2 tsp black pepper

Method:

1. Preheat your air fryer to 400°F.
2. Pat the chicken thighs dry with paper towels and place them in a large bowl.
3. Drizzle the olive oil over the chicken and toss to coat. Then sprinkle on the garlic powder, paprika, salt, and pepper, and rub the seasoning all over the thighs.

4. Arrange the seasoned chicken thighs in a single layer in the air fryer basket, making sure they aren't touching.
5. Air fry for 18-22 minutes, flipping the thighs halfway through, until the skin is crispy and the internal temperature reaches 165°F.
6. Remove the air fryer chicken thighs from the basket and let them rest for 5 minutes before serving. Enjoy!

Tips:

- For extra crispy skin, pat the chicken very dry before seasoning.
- Try different seasoning blends like lemon-pepper, Cajun, or Italian.
- Brush the chicken with a little honey or BBQ sauce towards the end for a tasty glaze.
- Air fry the chicken in batches if needed to avoid overcrowding the basket.

- Reheat any leftovers in the air fryer for 3-4 minutes to recrisp the skin.

AIR FRYER BEEF MEATBALLS

Ingredients:

- 1 lb ground beef
- 1/2 cup breadcrumbs
- 1/4 cup grated parmesan
- 1 egg
- 2 garlic cloves, minced
- 1 tsp dried oregano
- 1 tsp salt
- 1/2 tsp black pepper

Method:

1. Preheat your air fryer to 400°F.
2. In a large bowl, gently mix together the ground beef, breadcrumbs, parmesan, egg, garlic, oregano, salt, and pepper until just combined. Be careful not to overmix.

3. Scoop out the mixture by the tablespoonful and roll into 1-inch meatballs.
4. Arrange the meatballs in a single layer in the air fryer basket, making sure they aren't touching.
5. Air fry for 10-12 minutes, flipping halfway through, until the meatballs are cooked through and browned on the outside.
6. Serve the air fryer beef meatballs immediately, either as a main dish or as an appetizer with your favorite dipping sauces.

Tips:

- For even more flavor, try adding chopped onion, fresh herbs, or spices to the meatball mixture.
- After shaping, you can refrigerate the meatballs for up to 24 hours before air frying.

- Air fry the meatballs in batches to avoid overcrowding the basket.
- Leftovers can be reheated in the air fryer for 3-4 minutes.

AIR FRYER PORK CHOPS

Ingredients:

- 4 boneless pork chops, about 1-inch thick
- 2 tbsp olive oil
- 1 tsp garlic powder
- 1 tsp paprika
- 1 tsp salt
- 1/2 tsp black pepper

Method:

1. Preheat your air fryer to 400°F.
2. Pat the pork chops dry with paper towels and place them in a shallow baking dish or plate.
3. In a small bowl, mix together the olive oil, garlic powder, paprika, salt, and pepper. Brush or rub this seasoning mixture all

over the pork chops, coating them evenly on both sides.

4. Arrange the seasoned pork chops in a single layer in the air fryer basket, making sure they aren't touching.

5. Air fry for 12-16 minutes, flipping the pork chops halfway through, until they reach an internal temperature of 145°F.

6. Remove the air fryer pork chops from the basket and let them rest for 5 minutes before serving.

Tips:

- For extra crispy pork chops, pat them very dry before seasoning.
- Try different seasoning blends like Cajun, lemon-pepper, or Italian.
- Brush the pork chops with a little honey or BBQ sauce towards the end for a tasty glaze.
- Air fry the pork chops in batches if needed to avoid overcrowding the basket.

- Reheat any leftovers in the air fryer for
  3-4 minutes to recrisp the exterior.

AIR FRYER STEAK FAJITAS

Ingredients:

- 1 lb flank steak, thinly sliced against the
  grain
- 2 bell peppers, sliced into strips
- 1 onion, sliced into strips
- 2 tbsp olive oil
- 2 tsp fajita seasoning
- 1 tsp garlic powder
- Salt and pepper to taste
- Tortillas, guacamole, salsa, etc. for serving

Method:

1. Preheat your air fryer to 400°F.
2. In a large bowl, toss the sliced steak, bell
   peppers, and onions with the olive oil,
   fajita seasoning, garlic powder, salt, and
   pepper until everything is evenly coated.

3. Spread the steak and veggie mixture in an even layer in the air fryer basket.
4. Air fry for 12-15 minutes, tossing halfway through, until the steak is cooked through and the veggies are tender and charred on the edges.
5. Serve the air fryer steak fajitas immediately, with warm tortillas, guacamole, salsa, and any other desired toppings.

Tips:

- For best results, use a flavorful steak like flank, skirt, or hanger steak.
- Cut the steak against the grain for maximum tenderness.
- Feel free to adjust the seasoning amounts to suit your taste preferences.
- Air fry the steak and veggies in batches if needed to avoid overcrowding.
- Reheat any leftovers in the air fryer for 3-4 minutes.

AIR FRYER SHRIMP SCAMPI

Ingredients:

- 1 lb large shrimp, peeled and deveined
- 4 tbsp unsalted butter, melted
- 3 garlic cloves, minced
- 1/4 cup dry white wine
- 2 tbsp lemon juice
- 1 tsp dried parsley
- 1/4 tsp red pepper flakes (optional)
- Salt and pepper to taste
- Lemon wedges, for serving

Method:

1. Preheat your air fryer to 400°F.
2. In a medium bowl, toss the shrimp with the melted butter, garlic, white wine, lemon juice, parsley, and red pepper flakes (if using). Season with salt and pepper.
3. Spread the shrimp mixture in an even layer in the air fryer basket.

4. Air fry for 6-8 minutes, shaking the basket halfway, until the shrimp are pink, curled, and cooked through.
5. Remove the air fryer shrimp scampi from the basket and serve immediately, with lemon wedges on the side.

Tips:

- Use large, jumbo-sized shrimp for the best texture.
- Be careful not to overcrowd the air fryer basket - cook the shrimp in batches if needed.
- Serve the air fryer shrimp scampi over pasta, zucchini noodles, or with crusty bread to soak up the delicious sauce.
- Sprinkle it with extra parsley or lemon zest for extra flavor.
- Reheat any leftovers in the air fryer for 2-3 minutes.

AIR FRYER CHICKEN PARMESAN

Ingredients:

- 4 boneless, skinless chicken breasts, pounded thin
- 1 cup panko breadcrumbs
- 1/2 cup grated Parmesan cheese
- 1 tsp Italian seasoning
- 1/2 tsp garlic powder
- 1/4 tsp salt
- 1/4 tsp black pepper
- 2 eggs, beaten
- 1 cup marinara sauce
- 1 cup shredded mozzarella cheese

Method:

1. Preheat your air fryer to 380°F.
2. In a shallow bowl, combine the panko, Parmesan, Italian seasoning, garlic powder, salt, and pepper.

3. Dip the chicken breasts in the beaten egg, then dredge them in the breadcrumb mixture, pressing to help it adhere.
4. Arrange the breaded chicken in a single layer in the air fryer basket, making sure they don't touch.
5. Air fry for 12-15 minutes, flipping halfway, until the chicken is golden brown and cooked through, reaching an internal temperature of 165°F.
6. Top the air fried chicken with the marinara sauce and shredded mozzarella cheese.
7. Air fry for an additional 2-3 minutes, until the cheese is melted and bubbly.
8. Serve the air fryer chicken parmesan immediately, garnished with fresh basil or parsley if desired.

Tips:

- For extra crispy chicken, spray the breaded chicken lightly with cooking spray before air frying.

- Adjust cooking time as needed for thicker or thinner chicken breasts.
- Serve over pasta, zucchini noodles, or with a fresh salad for a complete meal.
- Reheat leftovers in the air fryer for 3-4 minutes to recrisp the chicken.

AIR FRYER PORK TENDERLOIN

Ingredients:

- 1 lb pork tenderloin, trimmed of silver skin
- 2 tbsp olive oil
- 1 tsp garlic powder
- 1 tsp onion powder
- 1 tsp dried thyme
- 1 tsp salt
- 1/2 tsp black pepper

Method:

1. Preheat your air fryer to 400°F.

2. Pat the pork tenderloin dry with paper towels and place in a shallow dish or baking sheet.
3. In a small bowl, combine the olive oil, garlic powder, onion powder, thyme, salt, and pepper. Rub this seasoning mixture all over the pork tenderloin, coating it evenly.
4. Place the seasoned pork tenderloin in the air fryer basket, making sure it doesn't touch the sides.
5. Air fry for 15-20 minutes, flipping halfway, until the pork reaches an internal temperature of 145°F.
6. Remove the air fryer pork tenderloin and let it rest for 5 minutes before slicing.
7. Slice the pork tenderloin into 1-inch thick slices and serve immediately.

Tips:

- For a crispier exterior, spray the pork with a light coating of cooking spray before air frying.

- Adjust the cooking time as needed based on the thickness of your pork tenderloin.
- Let the pork rest for 5 minutes before slicing to allow the juices to redistribute.
- Serve the air fryer pork tenderloin with your favorite sides like roasted vegetables, mashed potatoes, or a fresh salad.
- Reheat any leftovers in the air fryer for 3-4 minutes.

AIR FRYER
VEGETABLE SIDES

AIR FRYER BRUSSELS SPROUTS

Ingredients:

- 1 lb brussels sprouts, trimmed and halved
- 2 tablespoons olive oil or avocado oil
- 1 teaspoon garlic powder
- 1/2 teaspoon salt
- 1/4 teaspoon black pepper

Method:

1. Start by prepping the brussels sprouts. Trim off the woody ends, then slice any large sprouts in half so they're all a similar size. This helps them cook evenly.
2. Place the trimmed and halved brussels sprouts in a large bowl. Drizzle them with the olive oil or avocado oil and sprinkle on the garlic powder, salt, and pepper. Use your hands to toss and coat the sprouts evenly with the oil and seasonings.
3. Preheat your air fryer to 400°F.

4. Once heated, carefully place the seasoned brussels sprouts in the air fryer basket in a single, even layer. You may need to work in batches depending on the size of your air fryer.
5. Air fry the brussels sprouts for 8-12 minutes, shaking the basket halfway through, until they're crispy and caramelized on the outside and tender on the inside.
6. Keep an eye on them as they cook, and adjust the time up or down as needed based on the size of your brussels sprouts and your particular air fryer model. You want them to be crispy but not burnt.
7. Once the air fryer brussels sprouts are done, remove the basket and transfer the sprouts to a serving dish.
8. You can leave them as-is, or toss them with a sprinkle of parmesan cheese, a squeeze of lemon juice, or a few crumbles of crispy bacon.

9. Serve the air fried brussels sprouts immediately, while they're hot and crispy.

AIR FRYER ASPARAGUS

Ingredients:

- 1 lb fresh asparagus, tough ends trimmed
- 1 tbsp olive oil or avocado oil
- 1 tsp garlic powder
- 1/2 tsp salt
- 1/4 tsp black pepper

Method:

1. Preheat your air fryer to 400°F.
2. In a large bowl, toss the trimmed asparagus spears with the olive oil, garlic powder, salt, and pepper until evenly coated.
3. Arrange the seasoned asparagus in a single layer in the air fryer basket, making sure the spears aren't overlapping.
4. Air fry for 8-12 minutes, shaking the basket halfway through, until the

asparagus is tender-crisp and the tips are lightly browned.

5. Cooking time may vary depending on the thickness of your asparagus spears and your particular air fryer model, so keep an eye on it and adjust the time as needed.

6. Once the air fryer asparagus is done, immediately transfer it to a serving dish.

7. Optionally, you can squeeze a bit of lemon juice over the top and garnish with freshly grated parmesan cheese.

Tips:

- For even crispier asparagus, give the spears a light misting of cooking spray before air frying.
- Try using different dried herbs and spices like Italian seasoning, smoked paprika, or red pepper flakes.
- Adjust the cooking time based on how crisp or tender you like your asparagus.

Thinner spears may need a minute or two less.
- Serve the air fryer asparagus as a simple side dish, or toss it with pasta, eggs, or your favorite proteins.
- Reheat any leftovers in the air fryer for 2-3 minutes to maintain the crispy texture.

AIR FRYER SWEET POTATO FRIES

Ingredients:

- 2 lbs sweet potatoes, peeled and cut into 1/2-inch thick fry shapes
- 2 tbsp olive oil or avocado oil
- 1 tsp garlic powder
- 1 tsp paprika
- 1/2 tsp salt
- 1/4 tsp black pepper

Method:

1. Preheat your air fryer to 400°F.
2. In a large bowl, toss the sweet potato fry shapes with the olive oil, garlic powder,

paprika, salt, and pepper until evenly coated.

3. Working in batches if needed, arrange the seasoned sweet potato fries in a single layer in the air fryer basket, making sure they're not overlapping.

4. Air fry for 12-16 minutes, shaking the basket halfway through, until the fries are crispy and golden brown.

5. The exact cooking time may vary depending on the thickness of your fries and your specific air fryer model, so keep an eye on them and adjust the time as needed.

6. Once the air fryer sweet potato fries are done, immediately transfer them to a serving bowl or plate.

7. Serve the crispy sweet potato fries hot, with your favorite dipping sauces like ranch, honey mustard, or ketchup.

Tips:

- For even crispier fries, give them a light spritz of cooking spray before air frying.
- Try different seasoning blends - cajun, chili lime, or Italian herbs all work great.
- Cut the sweet potato fries to a uniform thickness so they cook evenly.
- Work in batches to avoid overcrowding the air fryer basket.
- Reheat any leftovers in the air fryer for 2-3 minutes to re-crisp them.

AIR FRYER CAULIFLOWER

Ingredients:

- 1 head of cauliflower, cut into bite-sized florets
- 2 tbsp olive oil or avocado oil
- 1 tsp garlic powder
- 1 tsp paprika
- 1/2 tsp salt
- 1/4 tsp black pepper

Method:

1. Preheat your air fryer to 400°F.
2. In a large bowl, toss the cauliflower florets with the olive oil, garlic powder, paprika, salt, and pepper until evenly coated.
3. Working in batches if needed, arrange the seasoned cauliflower in a single layer in the air fryer basket. Make sure the florets aren't overlapping.
4. Air fry for 12-15 minutes, shaking the basket halfway through, until the cauliflower is tender and lightly browned on the edges.
5. The exact cooking time may vary depending on the size of your cauliflower florets and your particular air fryer model, so keep an eye on it and adjust as needed.
6. Once the air fryer cauliflower is done, immediately transfer it to a serving bowl.
7. Optionally, you can toss the hot cauliflower with a sprinkle of grated

parmesan cheese, a squeeze of lemon juice, or some chopped fresh parsley.

Tips:

- For extra crispy cauliflower, spritz the florets with a light coating of cooking spray before air frying.
- Try different seasoning blends like Cajun, Italian, or ranch for variety.
- Cut the cauliflower into evenly sized florets so they cook uniformly.
- Work in batches to avoid overcrowding the air fryer basket.
- Reheat any leftovers in the air fryer for 2-3 minutes to re-crisp them.

AIR FRYER BROCCOLI

Ingredients:

- 1 head of broccoli
- Some olive oil or other cooking oil
- A pinch of salt
- A sprinkle of pepper

Method:

1. First, get a head of broccoli and cut it up into little tree-shaped pieces. Make sure the pieces are all about the same size so they cook evenly.
2. Put the broccoli pieces in a bowl. Drizzle a small amount of oil over them - just enough to lightly coat the broccoli. Then sprinkle on a pinch of salt and a little bit of pepper. Use your hands to gently toss the broccoli around so all the pieces get coated in the oil and seasonings.
3. Next, take the seasoned broccoli and put it into the air fryer basket. Spread the pieces out in a single layer so they're not all piled on top of each other.
4. Turn on the air fryer and set it to 400^0F. Let the broccoli cook for 8-12 minutes, shaking the basket halfway through.
5 When the time is up, your air fryer broccoli should be tender on the inside and a little crispy on the outside. Carefully

take the basket out of the air fryer and transfer the broccoli to a plate or bowl.

6. Serve the air fryer broccoli hot, maybe with a little extra salt and pepper on top if you want.

AIR FRYER GREEN BEANS

Ingredients:

- 1 pound of fresh green beans
- 1-2 tablespoons of olive oil or vegetable oil
- A pinch of salt
- A sprinkle of pepper

Method:

1. First, wash the green beans and trim off the ends. You want to end up with nice, straight green bean pieces that are all about the same length.
2. Put the trimmed green beans in a bowl. Drizzle a small amount of oil over them - just enough to lightly coat the beans. Then

sprinkle on a pinch of salt and a light sprinkle of pepper. Use your hands to gently toss the green beans around so they all get coated in the oil and seasonings.

3. Next, take the seasoned green beans and dump them into the air fryer basket. Spread the beans out in a single layer so they aren't piled up on top of each other.

4. Turn on the air fryer and set the temperature to 400 degrees Fahrenheit. Let the green beans cook for 8-12 minutes, shaking the basket halfway through to help them cook evenly.

5. When the time is up, your air fryer green beans should be tender and a little bit crispy on the outside. Carefully take the basket out of the air fryer and transfer the green beans to a serving dish.

6. You can serve the air fryer green beans just like that, or you can give them a little extra seasoning if you want - maybe a squeeze of lemon juice or a sprinkle of

grated parmesan cheese. Enjoy your crispy, flavorful green beans.

AIR FRYER ROASTED POTATOES

Ingredients:

- 3-4 medium potatoes
- 2-3 tablespoons olive oil or vegetable oil
- 1 teaspoon garlic powder
- 1 teaspoon paprika
- 1/2 teaspoon salt
- 1/4 teaspoon black pepper

Instructions:

1. First, wash the potatoes and cut them into 1-inch cubes. Try to make the potato cubes all about the same size so they cook evenly.
2. Put the potato cubes in a bowl. Drizzle the oil over them and use your hands to toss the potatoes around so they're all coated in the oil.

3. Next, sprinkle the garlic powder, paprika, salt, and pepper over the potatoes. Toss the potatoes again to make sure the seasonings are evenly distributed.

4. Now, take the seasoned potato cubes and spread them out in a single layer in the air fryer basket. Try not to overcrowd them.

5. Set the air fryer to 400°F and let the potatoes cook for 15-20 minutes. Every 5 minutes or so, open the air fryer and shake the basket to help the potatoes cook evenly.

6. When the time is up, the potatoes should be crispy on the outside and tender on the inside. Use tongs or a spoon to carefully remove the roasted potatoes from the air fryer.

7. Serve the air fryer roasted potatoes hot, maybe with a sprinkle of extra salt and pepper on top. You can also try mixing in some fresh chopped herbs like rosemary or thyme for extra flavor.

AIR FRYER EGGPLANT FRIES

Ingredients:

- 1 medium eggplant
- 2 tablespoons olive oil or vegetable oil
- 1 teaspoon garlic powder
- 1 teaspoon Italian seasoning
- 1/2 teaspoon salt
- 1/4 teaspoon black pepper

Method:

1. First, wash the eggplant and cut it into long, thin fry-shaped pieces. Try to make the fries all about the same thickness so they cook evenly.
2. Put the eggplant fry pieces in a bowl. Drizzle the oil over them and use your hands to toss the fries around until they're all coated in the oil.
3. Next, sprinkle the garlic powder, Italian seasoning, salt, and pepper over the oiled

eggplant fries. Toss them again to make sure the seasonings are distributed evenly.

4. Take the seasoned eggplant fries and spread them out in a single layer in the air fryer basket. Try not to overcrowd them.

5. Set the air fryer temperature to 400°F and let the eggplant fries cook for 12-15 minutes. Every 5 minutes or so, open the air fryer and give the basket a shake to help the fries cook evenly.

6. When the time is up, the eggplant fries should be crispy on the outside and tender on the inside. Use tongs or a spoon to carefully remove the air fryer eggplant fries from the basket.

7. Serve the eggplant fries hot, maybe with a sprinkle of extra salt and pepper or a dipping sauce on the side.

AIR FRYER

DESSERTS

AIR FRYER APPLE PIE BITES

Ingredients:

- 1 package of refrigerated pie crust
- 2 medium apples, peeled, cored and diced
- 2 tablespoons brown sugar
- 1 teaspoon ground cinnamon
- 1 tablespoon butter, melted
- Powdered sugar for dusting (optional)

Method:

1. First, unroll the pie crust dough and use a rolling pin to flatten it out a bit. Then use a round cookie cutter or the rim of a glass to cut the dough into small circular shapes, like little pie crusts.
2. In a bowl, mix together the diced apples, brown sugar, and cinnamon until the apples are coated.
3. Take a dough circle and put about 1 2 teaspoons of the apple mixture in the center. Fold the dough over to make a

little half-moon shape and crimp the edges with a fork to seal it.

4. Repeat this with the remaining dough and apple filling to make as many little apple pie bites as you can.

5. Brush the tops of the sealed pie bites with the melted butter.

6. Carefully place the apple pie bites in a single layer in your air fryer basket. You may need to cook them in batches depending on the size of your air fryer.

7. Air fry the bites at 350°F for 8-10 minutes, flipping them halfway through, until they're golden brown.

8. Remove the cooked air fryer apple pie bites from the basket and let them cool for a couple minutes. Then, if desired, dust them lightly with powdered sugar.

9. Serve the warm, crispy air fryer apple pie bites and enjoy! They're a delicious little bite-sized treat.

AIR FRYER DONUTS

Ingredients:

- 1 can (16.3 oz) refrigerated buttermilk biscuit dough
- 2 tablespoons granulated sugar
- 1 teaspoon ground cinnamon
- 2 tablespoons unsalted butter, melted

Method:

1. Open the can of biscuit dough and separate the individual biscuits. Use your fingers to gently poke a hole in the center of each biscuit to create a donut shape.
2. In a small bowl, mix together the granulated sugar and ground cinnamon to make the cinnamon-sugar coating.
3. Preheat your air fryer to 350°F.
4. Working in batches if needed, carefully place the donut shaped biscuits in a single layer in the air fryer basket, making sure they don't touch each other.

5. Air fry the donuts for 5-6 minutes, flipping them over halfway through the cooking time. The donuts should be golden brown when done.
6. Remove the cooked air fryer donuts from the basket and immediately brush the tops and sides with the melted butter.
7. While the donuts are still warm, roll them in the cinnamon-sugar mixture, gently coating all sides.
8. Serve the warm, coated air fryer donuts immediately. The outsides should be crispy while the insides remain soft and fluffy.
9. Repeat the process with the remaining donut dough, working in batches as needed.

AIR FRYER CHURROS

Ingredients:

- 1 cup water
- 2 tbsp white sugar

- 1/2 tsp salt
- 1 cup all-purpose flour
- 2 eggs
- Vegetable oil spray
- 1/2 cup white sugar
- 1 tsp ground cinnamon

Method:

1. First, in a pot, heat up some water with a couple tablespoons of sugar and a pinch of salt. Bring this to a boil.
2. Once boiling, take the pot off the heat and stir in the flour until a thick dough forms. Let this dough cool for 5 minutes.
3. Then, add the eggs one at a time, stirring really well after each one, until the dough is smooth.
4. Scoop the churro dough into a piping bag with a big star-shaped tip.
5. Spray the air fryer basket with some cooking spray.

6. Pipe the churro dough directly into the air fryer basket, cutting it into 4-5 inch long pieces with scissors.

7. Air fry the churros at 400°F for 8-10 minutes, flipping them halfway through, until they're golden brown.

8. In a bowl, mix together some more sugar and cinnamon.

9. As soon as the churros come out of the air fryer, roll them in the cinnamon-sugar mixture to coat them.

AIR FRYER CHOCOLATE CHIP COOKIES

Ingredients:

- 1 cup (2 sticks) unsalted butter, softened
- 3/4 cup granulated sugar
- 3/4 cup brown sugar
- 1 egg
- 2 tsp vanilla extract
- 2 1/4 cups all-purpose flour
- 1 tsp baking soda

- 1/2 tsp salt
- 1 cup semi-sweet chocolate chips

Instructions:

1. First, get a large bowl and use a hand mixer or spoon to beat the softened butter together with the granulated sugar and brown sugar until it's smooth and creamy.
2. Next, beat in the egg and vanilla extract.
3. In a separate bowl, whisk together the flour, baking soda, and salt.
4. Slowly mix the dry ingredients into the wet ingredients until just combined, then fold in the chocolate chips.
5. Scoop the cookie dough into balls, about 2 tablespoons of dough per cookie.
6. Preheat your air fryer to 350°F.
7. Place the cookie dough balls in a single layer in the air fryer basket, making sure they don't touch.
8. Air fry for 6-8 minutes, until the cookies are golden brown on the edges.

9. Carefully remove the cookies from the air fryer and let them cool on the basket for 5 minutes before transferring to a wire rack.

AIR FRYER CINNAMON ROLLS

Ingredients:

- 1 can (13.8 oz) refrigerated cinnamon roll dough
- 1 tbsp melted butter

Icing:

- 2 oz cream cheese, softened
- 1/4 cup powdered sugar
- 1 tbsp milk

Method:

1. First, open up the can of cinnamon roll dough and separate the individual rolls.
2. Place the cinnamon rolls in a single layer in the air fryer basket, making sure they don't touch each other.

3. Brush the tops of the cinnamon rolls with the melted butter.

4. Air fry the cinnamon rolls at 320°F for 8-10 minutes, until they're puffed up and golden brown on top.

5. While the cinnamon rolls are cooking, make the icing. In a small bowl, use a spoon to mix together the softened cream cheese, powdered sugar, and milk until smooth and creamy.

6. Once the cinnamon rolls are done, carefully remove them from the air fryer.

7. Drizzle the cream cheese icing over the warm cinnamon rolls, making sure to get it in all the nooks and crannies.

8. Serve the air fryer cinnamon rolls warm and enjoy their gooey, cinnamony deliciousness!

AIR FRYER FUNNEL CAKES

Ingredients:

- 1 cup all-purpose flour

- 2 tablespoons white sugar
- 1 teaspoon baking powder
- 1/4 teaspoon salt
- 1 egg
- 3/4 cup milk
- 1 teaspoon vanilla extract
- Vegetable oil spray
- Powdered sugar for dusting

Method:

1. In a medium bowl, whisk together the flour, sugar, baking powder, and salt.
2. In a separate small bowl, whisk together the egg, milk, and vanilla extract.
3. Slowly pour the wet ingredients into the dry ingredients and whisk until a smooth, pourable batter forms. The consistency should be like pancake batter.
4. Lightly spray the air fryer basket with vegetable oil.

5. Working in batches, pour the batter into a funnel or squeeze the bottle with a small round opening.

6. Swirl the batter in a circular motion to create a spiral shape as you squeeze it into the air fryer basket.

7. Air fry the funnel cakes at 370°F for 4-5 minutes, until golden brown.

8. Carefully remove the funnel cakes from the air fryer basket and place on a plate or cooling rack.

9. While still warm, dust the funnel cakes generously with powdered sugar.

10. Serve the air fryer funnel cakes immediately, while they're hot and crispy.

AIR FRYER S'MORES

Ingredients:

- Graham cracker squares
- Marshmallows
- Chocolate squares (like Hershey's)

Method:

1. Preheat your air fryer to 400°F.
2. Take a graham cracker square and place a chocolate square on top of it.
3. Top the chocolate with a marshmallow.
4. Place the s'mores assembly in the air fryer basket in a single layer, making sure the pieces don't touch.
5. Air fry the s'mores for 2-3 minutes, keeping a close eye on them, until the marshmallows are golden brown and puffed up.
6. Carefully remove the air fryer s'mores from the basket and top each one with another graham cracker square to make a sandwich.
7. The chocolate should be melted and the marshmallow should be gooey and toasted.
8. Enjoy the warm, melty air fryer s'mores right away! You can also let them cool for

a minute or two before eating if you prefer.

AIR FRYER BAKED APPLES

Ingredients:

- 4 medium-sized apples (such as Honeycrisp, Gala, or Fuji)
- 1/4 cup brown sugar
- 1 teaspoon ground cinnamon
- 2 tablespoons unsalted butter, cubed
- 2 tablespoons chopped walnuts or pecans (optional)

Instructions:

1. Preheat your air fryer to 350°F.
2. Wash and core the apples, making sure to leave the bottom intact so the filling doesn't leak out. Use a melon baller or spoon to scoop out the core, leaving about 1/2 inch at the bottom.
3. In a small bowl, mix together the brown sugar and cinnamon.

4. Stuff each cored apple evenly with the brown sugar-cinnamon mixture. Top each apple with a few cubes of butter.
5. If using, sprinkle the chopped nuts over the top of the apples.
6. Carefully place the stuffed apples in the air fryer basket, making sure they don't touch each other.
7. Air fry the apples for 18-22 minutes, until they are tender when pierced with a fork and the skins are starting to wrinkle.
8. Remove the baked apples from the air fryer and let them cool for 5 minutes before serving.
9. Serve the air fryer baked apples warm, with the delicious cinnamon-sugar sauce spooned over the top. Top with a scoop of vanilla ice cream, if desired.

CONCLUSION

SUMMARY OF AIR FRYER BENEFITS

Air fryers are pretty great for a few key reasons:

1. First off, they're a lot healthier than regular frying. Since they use hot air circulation instead of oil, you can make crispy fried foods with way less fat and calories.

2. They're also super fast and easy to use. Air fryers heat up quickly and cook things in half the time of a normal oven. And cleanup is a breeze since there's hardly any messy oil or grease.

3. But air fryers aren't just good for frying - you can use them to bake, roast, and even make desserts like the ones we talked about. They're really versatile little appliances.

4. Another nice thing is that air fryers are pretty energy efficient compared to full-size ovens. So you can save some

money on your electricity bill when you use one.

5. And lastly, air fryers have a nice compact design that takes up way less counter space than a lot of other kitchen gadgets. Super convenient for small kitchens.

Made in the USA
Columbia, SC
12 July 2024

38534017R00059